THE PRIME ANNIVERSARY

JAY WRIGHT

FLOOD EDITIONS

CHICAGO

THE PRIME ANNIVERSARY

2019

THE PRIME ANNIVERSARY

ὦ καλή ὦ χαρίεσσα

Truth: names travel a watery route to heaven,
so says Concha Méndez, or so she would have said,
if she had any regard for physics. Seven
witnesses report that ether surely has failed,
a small erasure hardly noticed at Quito;
lines in that atmosphere seem to circle and flow
tangent to themselves. What does geometry know?

———————

μὲν βάσις ἀγλαΐας ἀρχά a perfect pitch
and revelation, a neutralino on its
haunch. Someone has proposed the baptismal limits
of Sekkaku-an, and has heard the hemistich
sounding the absolute zero of time. Such cold
transparent matter sits lightly on the threshold,
a hermitage of nothing, nothing can withhold.

———————

4

Alberti knows that essential rhythm, that string
of bound forms he returned to Gádir with his paint,
brushes, and definitive sketches, and his saint-
trammeled Buenos Aires politics, the blue spring
of it matched only by his faith in olive Spain.
Consider him ποιητός a perfect chaplain
at ease with Empedocles in their own domain.

———————

November transfigures all divided cultures.
Bandiagara gardens, faithful to fissures,
gorges, must trust an incontinent calendar,
and solve the puzzle of sandy soil, and that feldspar
of plateau solitude. What can the river say
to the reddish-brown rock as it begins to play
among harmonies it refuses to display?

———————

Concha Méndez confronts a continuous set
of states. What could she have seen in the ragged shape
of lightning, in a solar prominence, the pet
intentions that will appear on every landscape?
Was it Ptolemy who advised us to beware
of a theoretical grasp without a fair
symmetry of practice, most rigorous and spare?

————

Alison reads Dante's stars, and finds a verbal
shadow midway to Paradise, the truth of it
in imagination, desire, integral
vocation the Carthaginian might permit.
Call this will, or memory, or a gift not quite
the double dance or double journey. Why rewrite
the poet's purple page then draw it out of sight?

————

Do not be astonished if you hear a drumming,
or meet an unattended leopard in the bush.
The mask—half in shadow, half in sunlight—will bring
you through death; you might think of this as pull and push
of an electron, orbiting its own demise.
We know our scholars speak too often in disguise,
embrace Abakuá, always sit to improvise.

———————

That periodic bouncing between mirror points
might define the note's order in the scale. Custom
could determine all that the spent soul might fathom,
make of it a blue galaxy that disappoints.
Consider a slow dance about an axis, dust
in an elliptical field. Now Emily must
go mad with her math, and take these errors in trust.

———————

Aristoxenus disturbs; he allows no strict
intention in motion, no voice without its space.
Cleonides defends himself with commonplace
notions of a point on a line, a derelict
argument, given body by fuzzy sequence.
Call upon Guillén, his radical confidence
in singing the world's blossoming transience.

———————

Propertius suffers his delightful withdrawal,
the Greek of it. That Epicurean structure
turns his head from space to time, brings him an impure
balance that will not disturb; just there such modal
properties find no comfort and perch in music.
Nothing overcomes the radiant iambic;
no one forgets the geometry of lyric.

———————

Third level (a): $2 \times 5 \times 7 = 70$

Even in dreams, hyssop refuses to appear,
refuses to forgive what sits upon this heart.
The persistent autumn unrolls from year to year.
Consider this finite expression a lost art.
Can the poet understand such an injury,
the melancholia he can never graph or plot?
Can he contribute to a latent conjury?
The hyssop always keeps its secrets, and will not
console the poet, troubled by the perfect silence,
and by the garden's exhaustive benevolence.

———————

In Pittsburgh, no Victorian ever suffers
a tropospheric complacency, or gets caught
in ice—always careful to avoid the vespers
of a mere "form of words." They say that Frege bought
a paradox that left him without a true soul
and exposed to the phased molecule of logic.
Why should those in Mali believe in the systole
and diastole of vernacular too caustic
as a testable state of affairs? We measure
demand for existence without hope of a cure.

———————

In Paris, Juan Larrea sits with the notion
of perfection, or perhaps we should say, the fact
of two bodies becoming one, braving the tact
of a disappearance, or bartered deception—
what we might find too formal, a blunt relation
that makes of Larrea a shadow with a voice.
Why think about these structural matters, the choice
of a variable without denotation?
Why sit grooming a French text, the intentional
second intention, sign of complete withdrawal?

———————

Frank Faucett plays cards with Leibniz, and there he learns
the Law of Continuity, but can never
understand the limiting case, or the merger
of methodologies that the point overturns
when a term goes fishing for semantic content.
Frank knows just where the fiction starts, the specific
intention of one who counts, the mathematic
ontology that will never seem consistent.
We will not deal with Galileo, or the Greek
with his diagrams and invisible critique.

———————

Baca likes to spin in familiar air, pretend
he has all he needs in uniform relation.
Mark Wilson gives him all due credit, and will lend
him support against any attenuation
of his being. Baca knows, by heart, that Leibniz
with his small quantities gives our physicists fits—
such a Galilean conspiracy, a shell
game of counting, separation, perhaps a spell
of ontology. Why argue with a fiction?
Why call a body's measure a contradiction?

———————

Marcel Duchamp hears a temporal displacement
in Tompkins Square, and dreams of the fourth dimension.
He will need a legisign, or an enhancement
that will escape his sensuous contemplation,
long before he has matter or force to propose.
He will not, of course, avoid this intensity
of field, or go right to left only to compose
another fuzzy border; such absurdity
never would appeal to his totemic nature.
All Cubists will continue to think him impure.

———————

Ogotemmêli stands on his own green terrace.
The lines and planes of that garden should remind him
of imaginary things, no finite and slim
number of his body's diagram, or slow pace
of a logical relation tuned in Athens.
Reviel will argue, deductive make-believe
might turn to aspiration, and construct an ens
that only pragmatic matter might so conceive.
Here there remains an indiscernible substance,
the weight of a moving body, fleeting instance.

———————

Third level (b): $2 \times 5 \times 7 = 70$

Góngora remains
displeased, the water binds him,
and Peter, fluid
as carved rock at a seacoast,
cradles every certitude.

Spyros sets the pot
astir in Miletus, rain
recalls a body
in Athens, a blue column
of a Montreal Sunday.

This magnetic field,
a fourth estate, effigy
set by tidal suns
leaves what cannot disappear
—a participating light.

The spherical monk
sees the sun's white effusion;
morning never grows
without the strict linear
occasion of darkest night.

Porcelain will not
insist upon wine from Prague,
or tea from Hunan;
shaggy evenings seem to wake
a democratic spirit.

————

Syndetic Lagos,
an ambiguous estate,
welcomes a stranger.

Molinari finds
the temper of his garden
can sustain a loss.

Think virtue of birds
in a stone bath, the winter
on a goldfinch wing.

Should hemlock shelter
the red in autumn sedum,
or welcome winter.

One sees a rose wall
in Pedregal, fictional,
afloat on gray air.

Circular movement
measures a triangular
world at once at rest.

A clock makes itself
of precious metals and glass
and a damaged star.

———————

Second level (a): $5 \times 7 = 35$

The yellow basin
in the corner, a line's brief
natural movement,
offers the clarified mind
a moment of perfect rest.

A conceptual
silence might only measure
the apple's soundness,
its red mathematical
temperate inclination.

Formal qualities
leave no space for shifty rule,
no room for storing
the hovering density
of law—number has no place.

The morning opens
on a secret spell, the smell
of snakeroot, the bees
tracing a diminished green
in flight, small token of peace.

Barcelona makes
a case for forgetfulness,
promises nothing
to a perfect construction:
sand and white flaming roses.

Franciscans propose
a sharp initiation.
Leibniz lies in wait,
his theological masque
already a chancy farce.

Think procedural
memory, its residue.
Let an ordered pair
repair a damaged design.
All bitter neurons taste sweet.

————————

Who will uncover
the geography of wine,
extensive, finite?

A corruptible
composition finds no place
unprepared, or set.

The playful German
plots a transcendental curve
and figured absence.

Underground, marble
starts its ascent to service,
though it hides its name.

Cum silentio
the saint waits on salvation.
Does she hear God's name?

————

Second level (b): $7 \times 5 = 35$

THE GEOMETRY OF RHYTHM

(A dark space. No movement. No sound. A sudden flood of variously colored lights turns the space into a warren of interconnected geometrical figures. There is a music stand to the left; a large manuscript paper, showing the letter "c," sits upon it. Bivio appears, wearing a choir robe. He produces claves and a small bell; carefully places the bell at his feet; begins to play the claves. He stops, mumbles or sings an unintelligible phrase, stops, repeats the process. Patterns in his performance begin to take shape. He sounds (/uu/u), then (/uu/uu), then (/uuu/u). We hear him say "glóriam túam." He looks astonished, hides within his patterns. He screams "dómine íbismus," looks astonished, once again hides.)

BIVIO

One does not sing so faithfully without a sense of the body. Dogma. The sanction of fussy clerks. I will not be constrained. *(Grogach, wearing rugby clothes, appears.)*

GROGACH

Constraint. Certainly a concept worth considering. Have you?

BIVIO

Have I what?

GROGACH

The solution to those lines.

BIVIO

I can always count upon you . . .

GROGACH

Ah, let's not go too fast, or too far. You mentioned that config-
uration of substance. *(Bivio stops his ears.)*

BIVIO

Please. You of all people should be well aware of that substance,
that "something we know not what."

GROGACH

Don't pretend to a composition you don't understand. Stick to
your music.

BIVIO

This is not music.

GROGACH

Then it's geometry. I meant to take this up with you. It seems to me that you have lost the architecture of meaning here.

BIVIO

Oh boy, I can see you've spent some time in the country with that ... what does he call himself now? ... that transitive relation.

GROGACH

It never fails. These rhetoricians think they can measure the production of their babbling as though they had created el pájaro en la mano.

BIVIO

My god. I won't let you get away with it this time.

GROGACH

This time!? What do you mean?

BIVIO

I mean, sir, that you have entered upon a serious inquiry. You see me here testing the limits of a material existence ... I repeat, a material existence ... and what do you do? You throw up an improbable composition of signs and intentions. And then try to get me to acknowledge the geometrical intention of a cow's leg in dung.

GROGACH

That does it. But I should thank you for reminding me how simple, and how simply, the world appears. So why should I care that you badmouth my mother, and try to make this little convocation we have here an esoteric thing that needs some number to exist?

BIVIO

There you go again. But I insist ... (*He attacks his claves again, calls out again, substituting "Dómino déo" for "glóriam túam."*)

GROGACH

What did you say?

BIVIO

Where?

GROGACH

There. Back up. That doesn't fit. A true mathematical intelligence would tell you that in a consistent system graphs lying on top of each other represent infinite solutions.

BIVIO

Let's not talk about this infinite person.

GROGACH

No. Let's not. You can't keep doing this.

BIVIO

And why not?

GROGACH

It's only singing within itself.

(They start, with Grogach chanting the rhythm that Bivio marks. They gradually wind down into silence. A solitary violin breaks the silence, sounding the Gypsy scale:

c   d   e♭   f♯   g   a♭   b   c¹

Bivio removes the letter "c" from the music stand, replaces it with the letter "d.")

BIVIO

So you caught me, did you? You look surprised. What can I tell you? The sound progresses. If that disturbs you, say that the notes move on their own volition, that they create a path for themselves by going forward. I won't get into that silly argument of possession that lowrider stirred up with his formal properties and formal relations. You would think the tonic as common as the second. Oh, forgive me. I forget that you have very little in the way of musical training.

GROGACH

Well, given all that, shall we make the appointment for the field?

BIVIO

My god, Grogach, we have infinite space for these small dis-
coveries. But there, if you want to remain idle, and stop your
ears to that next note . . .

GROGACH

Why, you have simply gone mad. Didn't I hear you invoking the
faithful body as I came up the road? Now, what do I hear? Some
silly prolongation that you can't even sustain.

BIVIO

Prolongation. Where did you get a word like that?

GROGACH

From the language of number, my friend.

BIVIO

Impossible. Oh, I see your trick, trying to slip your leopards by
me, dancing along a line that simply repeats itself.

GROGACH

I never repeat myself.

BIVIO

The line, Bruno, not you.

GROGACH

How can you make that distinction?

BIVIO

How can you chant my rhythm?

GROGACH

I do not enjoy your confusion, Bivio.

BIVIO

Have you ever heard of the fundamental entities, Love and Strife?

GROGACH

Another evasion.

BIVIO

Not at all. I have them in my Enchiridion. I keep all feigned appearances there.

GROGACH

Feigned?

BIVIO

Well made. Can't you understand?

GROGACH

Such variable instruction.

BIVIO

Did I sing you my khamruya, my wine poem?

GROGACH

Oh, my, the ascetic has discovered wine.

BIVIO

Will you pay attention? Wine represents forgetfulness. You should have encountered my blanched Frenchman who speaks of forgetfulness as vigilance. And that leads to a creative impulse, and every creative impulse recognizes death, and recognizes no bounds.

(Grogach removes the letter "d" from the stand, replaces it with "e♭." He walks briskly around Bivio, begins a dance movement that seems more of a martial arts maneuver than dance. He stops, confronts Bivio.)

GROGACH

Let's lower the pitch by a half step. I don't trust you, Bivio.

BIVIO

So you came in disguise.

GROGACH

I came prepared. Don't think I didn't have word of your Cubist intentions, out here chasing your own absence.

BIVIO

Whoa. You will have to draw me a picture of that notion, Grogach. My custom doesn't permit such understanding.

GROGACH

You tried to disarm me before. This subtle business with your altars and ceremonies.

BIVIO

Yes?

GROGACH

Look at you. There you stand, a point without a center.

BIVIO

I get it now. You atomists have given emptiness a new home, or a first home, or the possibility of a home, and you need regular, stoneass bodies to inhabit this embarrassment. Well, count me out.

GROGACH

Nay, sir, I will count you in. You will acknowledge that something compels you to remove yourself to this spot, and to construct a representation of yourself that soothes, that delights. Don't try to persuade me that you can walk away from your first-order ontology.

BIVIO

You accuse me, then, of having entered an unfamiliar region, where your sensuous enticements have no space, cannot take place.

GROGACH

Did I say that?

BIVIO

No, your body proposed it.

GROGACH

That faithful body that allows you to sing.

BIVIO

We seem to have come to a divide, or to a finite contest where my musico-rhetorical abilities can have no force. Did you come here to rescue me, Grogach?

GROGACH

I shouldn't have used that word, home.

BIVIO

Why not? What difference do these rocks make between the seafloor and the continents?

GROGACH

You know, Bivio, I believe that you believe in your disappearance, and that not even God could sketch your presence in his design.

BIVIO

I will have to sit down. *(Grogach sings an e♭.)* That won't accomplish a thing. Why don't you come, sit down, and let's start all over.

GROGACH

Sit on what rock?

BIVIO

The Aventine, the Palatine, the Quirinal.

GROGACH

Nonsense.

BIVIO

Well, sir, can I offer you this bit of sandstone, this bit of shale, or a touch of limestone? *(Grogach howls.)* What happened to that architecture of meaning?

GROGACH

Well, I thought we had something in common. But, no, you get tied up in your derivative simplicities.

BIVIO

Why you Kantian proposition, you! You insist on your privilege to insult me. *(The tritone, c d e♭, sounds three times.)*

GROGACH

So, Bivio. I never would have thought you'd sink so low as to propose your divinity.

BIVIO

What do you mean?

GROGACH

This breezy attempt to establish your place. Alright. I have no instrument. I float without substance. *(Bivio tries to console Grogach.)*

BIVIO

Listen to me, Grogach. Anyone listening to us would find it hard to distinguish between us. We don't need an extensive lexicon. We know what we know. And we needn't go sailing around looking for an extension of our properties. *(He gestures.)* Bivio. Grogach. What more do we need?

GROGACH

Well, you might find it easy to say that. You've put your finger on it. Grogach doesn't exist. Some idiot said you couldn't see me unless you saw me bouncing off you. And then he got off into some godawful confusion about counting and naming.

BIVIO

I know the man.

GROGACH

You can't know the man; he hasn't been invented yet ... constructed yet ... You know what I mean.

BIVIO

I do, I do. This reminds me of my friend, Johannes Kepler, who always questioned light as a substance existing independently.

GROGACH

You knew Kepler?

BIVIO

I did.

GROGACH

We can't keep up with your masks and ceremonies, your little predicational claims. I assume that you and the lowrider and the boy from Pittsburgh made up a gang. Pragmatists.

BIVIO

You have something against pragmatists?

GROGACH

Only that they have no real home, and seem too willing to live under laws that refuse formulation.

BIVIO

Well, well, well. My Grogach. Sound me that note again.

(Grogach tries his e♭. He and Bivio reach a moment of rest. Bivio takes away the e♭ paper, replaces it with one showing "f♯").

GROGACH

I told you I have no instrument.

BIVIO

I should have brought my oboe, my aulós. You think I just sit down here, day after day, banging away at my rhythm, a typical artist. You ought to understand this, Grogach. You with your numbers and accentual pleasantries, which have nothing at all to do with music. Did I say that? According to the initiate, such a phenomenon doesn't submit to number, and thereby might escape our senses.

GROGACH

I suppose I should understand this as the derivation of your European soul.

BIVIO

You might.

GROGACH

And your little sticks establish no more than a temporal order that your body understands.

BIVIO

Don't get tricky with me, Grogach. You think I've lost my voice? (*The four tones c, d, e♭, f♯ sound.*) Show your hands. (*Grogach does.*) There. That makes sense. No more of this usurpation.

GROGACH

Play me something.

BIVIO

I don't take requests.

GROGACH

I didn't think you did. I meant to hear the rhythm of your theology.

(Bivio packs his claves, makes to move away. Grogach makes an involuntary gesture to detain him, slowly withdraws his hand.)

BIVIO

You know why I would leave you, Grogach? Here? By yourself? *(Grogach nods, turns away.)* You didn't come up through that swamp, to reach me, and then have me run away. Speak to me, Grogach. Even you can't be satisfied with such an apostrophe.

GROGACH

You had in mind some justification?

BIVIO

Ah. Yes. I did open that box, didn't I?

GROGACH

You haven't noticed. *(He points at the music stand, where the letter "g" has replaced "f♯".)*

BIVIO

Of course, I noticed. I wanted to see if such a change made any difference to you.

GROGACH

Go on. Tell me about my failings.

BIVIO

That judgment doesn't appear in the box, Grogach. I don't contest what you have done, even if I could say what you have done, or might have done, to me. So. We seem to have agreed upon the fundamental nature of the world, this thing that never changes.

GROGACH

How in the world did you come to that?

BIVIO

How in the world, he says. *(He quotes.)* "But when I looked for the ultimate reasons for mechanism . . ."

GROGACH

Stop it! This playing with me.

BIVIO

There, you've hit upon it, one of the reasons I want to cut you loose. You've lost your sense of play. My Grogach would take advantage of this perturbation. But look at you, still caught in the orbit of some sensibility that you can't even define.

GROGACH

Good. Good. Bivio will tell me. Bivio has his justification wrapped up in some dead voice he can call upon when he wants. And yet Bivio thinks that I have no ear for his melographia.

BIVIO

Now, where did you get that?

GROGACH

I thought you'd get a kick out of some spiffy little instant you couldn't understand. Hey, what a pair we make. We go fishing at any moment for something that will last, and then we get pissed because the matter has escaped.

BIVIO

Stop it. You won't keep me here by taking over my voice. I have made up my mind that your canonical hours no longer concern me.

GROGACH

Bivio the migrant! He doesn't need a place.

BIVIO

We've gone over that ground.

GROGACH

We did not. We could never coordinate our disturbances. You see what I mean, this multiplicity of changing things, among which we, as you can see, might count.

BIVIO

I hadn't finished my justification, as you call it. You bring up your melographia, but you overlook how in my own rhythmographia I have given you a place that will not disappear because of your arithmetical and geometrical miscalculations.

GROGACH

I suppose I should pack my bags and go along with you.

BIVIO

Wake up, Grogach. We need this perfect moment of separation. Don't you see that?

GROGACH

I see that we have changed places.

BIVIO

No, no. We haven't got a place to exchange.

GROGACH

Make up your mind.

BIVIO

I mean within me.

GROGACH

How would I know that?

BIVIO

Yes, alright, I see now. You intend to hold me captive to my suffering. *(He quotes.)* "If I can call my suffering his Doing, my passion his Action …"

GROGACH

This won't work, Bivio. Haven't we done away with that first philosophy?

BIVIO

Now he wants to steal my music.

GROGACH

No. I simply don't want you to get away with what you've pulled on me before. In a minute, I'll look up, and we'll have an ambrosial spring at your feet, a different architecture to which I'll have to subject my spirit. No, Bivio, you have to retune your clock.

BIVIO

Retune. Did I discover you within me?

GROGACH

Listen, I've heard of this countable, nameable thing we call an individual. But must we sustain it?

(The five tones c, d, e♭, f♯, g sound all at once, then serially, then in various arpeggios, then fade gradually from the fifth to the tonic until there is no sound. Bivio grabs Grogach, rapidly frisks him.)

BIVIO

You and your associates made a mistake with me. I saw through you right from the start. You come here half undressed, pretending such innocence, such concern for the ascetic. *(He steps back.)* Give.

GROGACH

What? Give what?

BIVIO

The thing you use to order this performance. *(Grogach gathers himself to go.)*

GROGACH

Glóriam túam!

BIVIO

Stop it!

GROGACH

Ópera eíus! Ésse vidéatur! Don't look so astonished. We come from the same womb.

BIVIO

Don't talk to me about wombs. *(The "g" on the music stand has been replaced by "a♭.")*

GROGACH

You don't like such directness, do you? You would prefer a symbolic ontology, something with less force, something that lets us hide.

BIVIO

Ah, but the beautiful has no body.

GROGACH

We exist, Bivio.

BIVIO

I exist. You exist, if at all, as fiction.

GROGACH

Then why do you think I've come? Why do you think they sent me to you?

BIVIO

I have no idea. Perhaps they thought I'd give in, take you in. I won't point out the moment of weakness in that argument, a fault in your diagram, a failing in itself. I almost said in myself. You would have celebrated that mistake, wouldn't you? No more of this. Some part of us has to go. You go, Grogach; or I go. It has come to that.

GROGACH

Bivio. Bivio. Forgive me, but I simply can't take this preening seriously. I thought you had made it across. Earlier on, you called up a molecular design, and I thought, oh, god, he's got it. Do you know how that invigorated me? Assuming that distinction between you and me, which we need not recognize, because, as you say yourself, it doesn't exist.

BIVIO

I did *not* say that.

GROGACH

Well, bless me, I can trust my ears.

BIVIO

Your ears have got you in a fix. What does this have to do with that molecular design I supposedly conferred upon the world?

GROGACH

I understand, Bivio. We sometimes start an exploration we don't intend, and then we have to pull in our balls, or cover our ears, whatever you do in such matters. You want to recover yourself. But you cannot walk away, split us apart. There you stand in a new order. So. What do we need? A new definition.

BIVIO

Definition of what?

GROGACH

Of your body.

BIVIO

Go away, Grogach. I can't stand your breath.

GROGACH

Aha, my breath. Of course, you can see that, if I didn't breathe ...

BIVIO

Yes? Go on.

GROGACH

Nay, my man, I don't want to call attention to anything physical.

BIVIO

Like your diagrams.

GROGACH

You can say that. Fantastic how you seem to understand by refusing to understand. Look at me. *(He sings.)* "Three times seven, and that makes twenty-one ..." Progress, my man. I won't even josh you about mother nature, or about the constant heat it costs me just to keep breathing, to say nothing of reinventing you, or me, or us's, as the I's would have it. Don't disappear, Bivio, or the word will fall, and we won't have anything to mark this passage.

BIVIO

I knew I couldn't count upon your understanding.

GROGACH

Count. I can account for myself.

BIVIO

Where did that come from? Besides, that seems no more than an engineering misconception. *(The scale rehearses itself, but seemingly in disordered fashion.)* Don't you hear something funny there?

GROGACH

What do you mean?

BIVIO

The order, the order, Grogach.

GROGACH

I give up on you, Bivio. *(The "b" now replaces the "a♭" on the stand.)*

BIVIO

Tell me this doesn't disturb you, Grogach. This dancing from point to point, as though these sounds didn't refer to anything.

GROGACH

Of course they don't, Bivio. *(Bivio collars Grogach.)*

BIVIO

Let's start all over.

GROGACH

From nothing.

BIVIO

Yes, from nothing.

GROGACH

Then you'll have to take your arm from my throat. *(Bivio releases him.)* You didn't tell me that you cared so much about number. For a moment, I thought that they had made a mistake.

BIVIO

Let's leave them out of this.

GROGACH

We can't. We have to have their example to produce our own notation. I only agreed to leave them if they recognized my name and the path I would take, the way these little notes that now sit in our ears trace their own path. You can see that, can't you? *(The scale starts again, rapidly changing intervallic patterns.)*

BIVIO

Sound me that last note.

GROGACH

Oy, Bivio, the note has already sounded within you.

BIVIO

No. No sermons. *(Grogach takes up the bell, rings it vigorously. Bivio protests. Grogach dances, ringing the bell.)* Alright! Alright! *(Grogach stops.)* So you found your instrument.

GROGACH

And you found your faith.

BIVIO

Nonsense. I couldn't possibly go back to where I stood.

GROGACH

Exactly.

BIVIO

And neither could you. You can't now stand where I stood.

GROGACH

Exactly. Look, let's tear this place up. It has no shape.

BIVIO

Aha, so you fooled your masters. I suspect they suspected a disguise. They knew that when you arrived here, you would take a different tack. Oh, this business about your path. You simply had to get here, get in my skin, and then you could consider, or should I say discover, yourself on the path. May I ask you now—what will you do if this measure turns into a ghost?

GROGACH

You can't frighten me, Bivio. I have a way with my constituents.

BIVIO

I don't doubt it, since I number among them. *(The "$c^{\scriptscriptstyle 1}$" replaces the "b" on the stand.)*

GROGACH

I have learned to say—with Philolaus—that as long as sensible objects "have number" ... and then ... how does it go?

BIVIO

You brought it up, something about the substantial form of soul.

GROGACH

I said, right from the start, let's not go too far.

BIVIO

Certainly not. We'd lose the touch of duration.

GROGACH

I like that—the touch of duration. You know, after this extended conversation, I feel embarrassed to say that I admire the way you continue to surprise yourself. Just as now.

BIVIO

Please, Grogach. I feel twinned to your skills.

(The scale sounds in order c through c', pauses, then sounds from c' to c, then performs the rapid intervallic pattern, where all notes are used equally.)

Ring the bell, Grogach. Don't let them intimidate us. *(Grogach rings the bell; the scale repeats its performance at the same time.)*

GROGACH

Bivio, don't leave me on my own.

(Bivio forcefully plays his clave. All these figures clash, then settle into complementary patterns. A tuneful composition seems to surface, then disappear.)

BIVIO

What happened? What got us into that?

GROGACH

We had to make some adjustments.

BIVIO

Dream up a new configuration.

GROGACH

Exactly. Take another look at ourselves.

BIVIO

Each one.

GROGACH

Exactly.

BIVIO

After all, this could go on and on, forever.

GROGACH

Even though we set our own course.

BIVIO

We just had to assert ourselves.

GROGACH

Each one.

BIVIO

We had to make sure that everyone could understand the proposition, see the complete design.

GROGACH

I'd say that we have a thorough comedy here.

BIVIO

Well, we haven't gone to hell.

GROGACH

No, Bivio, I mean that nothing constrains us. Not your logic, not your faith, not your body.

(*The lights go out. In the dark, Bivio removes his robe, and Grogach puts it on. When the lights go up, Bivio is in rugby clothes, Grogach in Bivio's robe. Bivio has the bell; Grogach has the claves.*)

BIVIO

I haven't done much for you, have I?

GROGACH

Not at all. You've taught me the fragile geometry of self.

BIVIO

And you have taught me to live with my ambiguous rhythm.

GROGACH

Shall we exchange names?

BIVIO

Let's do.

(The scale goes into its performance. Grogach does the cursus rhythms. Bivio rings the bell, and improvises an unusual chant. A flood of the brightest light, then sudden darkness.)

JAY WRIGHT was born in Albuquerque, New Mexico in 1934 and spent his teens in San Pedro, California, where his father worked in the shipyards. After graduating from high school, he played for two minor-league ball clubs—Mexicali and Fresno—and spent a minute in spring training with the San Diego Padres of the old Pacific Coast League. He then served three years in the army, stationed in Germany. Thanks to the G.I. Bill, he received his B.A. in comparative literature from the University of California (Berkeley) and his M.A. from Rutgers University (New Brunswick). A jazz and música Latina bassist, he lives in Bradford, Vermont.

Wright is the author of fourteen previous books of poetry, and he has written more than forty plays and a dozen essays. A fellow of the American Academy of Arts and Sciences, his honors include a Guggenheim Fellowship, a Hodder Fellowship, a Lannan Literary Award for Poetry, a MacArthur Fellowship, and the Bollingen Prize for Poetry.